Nana's Garden Quilt

Mackie

Quilt Designed by Sharon Woo

a Quilt in a Day® Publication

This book is dedicated to the sisterhood of women, all warriors in His garden, who fight the good fight and give courage to those of us who can only hope and pray.

The authors' royalties will be donated to the American Cancer Society for breast cancer research.

First printing May, 1997
Published by Quilt in a Day®, Inc.
1955 Diamond St. San Marcos, CA 92069

©1997 by Mackie nee Jeanne Gretton and Sharon Woo

ISBN 0-922705-92-5

Editor Eleanor Burns
Assistant Editor Loretta Smith
Art Director Merritt Voigtlander
Production Assistant Robin Green

Table of Contents

Introduction

I t seems that all children have special names for their grandmothers. A lot depends on what words they are told to use and what they hear other people call them. Sharon called her maternal grandmother "Mama" as she did not want to be called "grandma." But Sharon's granddaughter, Brianna, calls Sharon "Nana," so now her grandson, Isiah, calls her that, too. And "Nana" is also what my children called their father's mother, hence the name of this quilt. They called my mother, "MeMa," but I don't know where they got the name… I called her "Ma." I don't know what I called my paternal grandmother. All I remember is that she was short, stout, and lived on a farm. I have vivid memories of the "outhouse."

I do remember my maternal grandmother, Margaret Cook, who was not short and didn't appear to be stout, though there was enough to provide cushiony hugs. She was from Ireland, County Cork, I believe, and brought with her all the superstitions, blarney, idiosyncrasies, and work ethic. She had a faith that sustained her through ten children, widowhood, and I can't remember how many grandchildren, of which I was one, being numbered among the black sheep variety.

Many a time I felt the tap-tap of her thimbled finger on my head when I had done something wrong, or hadn't done something right. She died when I was twelve, having lived the last years of her life in California with my widowed mother and her brood of three sons and two daughters—all hooligans, (according to her) with the exception of my sister, Miss Goodie Two-Shoes, and I say that with affection!

Mackie

"Gramma" and I shared a bedroom and the love of "praydees," (potatoes to you non-Irish) in any shape or form. Her fried ones were the best! I was a depression kid and we ate a lot of potatoes as well as bread which my mother baked. The dough provided baked biscuits and fried "doughgods" and "galligokeens," both of which were topped with Karo syrup.

Gramma taught me how to embroider by making dish towels from my mother's flour sacks. We would wash and hem them. On one corner we would iron on a transfer of Sunbonnet Sue depicting the chores to be done on all the days of the week. To this day I still look for one of those transfers from the thirties. I hesitate to tell you what I would do for one of them now!

Before my mother drove us to California in a 1929 Whippet (they said it would never make it to the outskirts of Minneapolis, Minnesota), Gramma divided her time among her nine children. One son was a Catholic priest. When she lived with us, I used to accompany her to the Holy Rosary church for all the masses, and all the night novenas, especially in the winter. I don't see how a small child would be of any assistance if she happened to fall, except to run for help. But I was willing, if only for the sweet reward on the way home. Gramma insisted we stop at the drugstore where she would dig in her pocketbook for her change purse to buy me candy. Neccos were my favorite, 'specially the licorice ones! Potatoes, bread, and candy! Is it any wonder I'm in the shape that I'm in! Plus all those genes!

When I was about eight, I remember mother cutting up one of Gramma's coats to make one for me. Believe me, it was heavy and wore like iron. Old heavy wool coats and pants were used for patchwork quilts. These were made for "blow, not for show."

My Gramma loved the roses and I loved the lilacs. Mom grew the sweetest smelling, biggest purple violets I ever saw. I used to carry them in the church processions. We had Cecil Bruner tea roses across the backyard, and every year we furnished the crown for the Blessed Virgin Mary statue at the Immaculate Conception church. We also provided the poinsettias at Christmas time. As organist, my mother provided the music for seventeen years, filling the church with beauty you could see, smell, and hear.

I don't think there is any greater reward than working in a garden, but teaching quilting sure runs a close second! I have planted a few quilt seeds these past ten years, and I've seen my students bloom. Their garden of quilts is a sight to behold!

Planting Your Nana's Garden

Fabric

When purchasing your fabric, select 100% cottons at least 42" wide that are consistently the same weight. Your "stash" of collected fabrics should also be the same weight. Upholstery fabrics are too heavy, knits too stretchy, and dress fabric too light. If the weight is less and differs slightly from the rest of the fabrics, try spraying with sizing to help balance it. If you can see your hand through the fabric, it should be discarded. Watch the weave. Loosely woven fabrics tend to fray because they do not have enough body. When sewn with other strips, a loose weave may warp the panel.

Color

You may choose any colors you like…

- ❖ all shades of one color and of one value
- ❖ selected shades and values
- ❖ all shades and varied values

  Lights, mediums and darks add interest and excitement, creating motion and themes.

Scrappy Cornerstones *(where four block corners meet)*

Cornerstones in a variety of scraps will blend with the rest of the pieces. If you want your cornerstones to stand out, select different fabrics but in the same color.

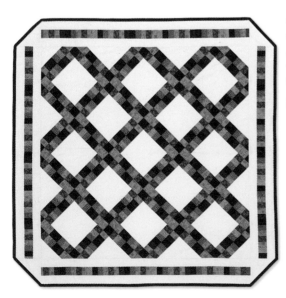

Planned Cornerstone Four-Patches

Planned Four-Patches require more care when putting the blocks together. Cornerstones of two different fabrics form the four-patch.

Background

Choose your background fabric carefully, based on what method you will use to personalize your quilt. A fine grain muslin or solid white is best for photo transfer, and is also suitable for free form machine quilting. A solid light color that coordinates with your strip fabrics can be very striking. Baby quilts can be personalized with pink background for a girl or blue for a boy. For a dramatically different look, try black background fabric and solid strip fabrics for an Amish theme.

A large graphic print or design, or a directional print requires special forethought (especially with planned cornerstones) because the blocks are set together "on point." Additionally, the quilt edges are half blocks and the quilt corners are quarter blocks.

Batting

There are different kinds of batting: natural fibers such as cotton or wool, and manmade fibers such as polyester. There are blends of both cotton and polyester. There are also different thicknesses of batt called "loft." The natural fibers are thin, while the polyesters can be as thin as the natural fibers, (6.6 ounce) to medium (12 to 16 ounce), or thick (20 to 24 ounce). They can be purchased in packages or bought by the yard from rolls. Machine quilting needs thin or medium batting. Free motion quilting should be with the thinner batts.

Backing

It's best if you purchase your backing after your quilt top is finished and measured.

Customizing Bed Size Quilts

The Yardage and Cutting charts are based on standard mattress sizes. The block portion of the quilt is planned to cover the mattress top. You may want more or fewer blocks depending on your mattress. The border portion of the quilt is planned to cover a 12" drop. If your mattress is thicker, you may wish to make adjustments in border widths to accommodate your measurements.

The approximate size listed on the Yardage chart is labeled "approximate" because seam sizes differ from quilter to quilter. Machine quilting also "shrinks" the size. The loft or thickness of the batting also makes a difference. It seems everything affects the overall size!

Customizing may change the amount of fabric needed for the quilt top, borders, backing and the batting. It is best to purchase the backing and batting after the quilt top is sewn together and has borders.

How Does Your Garden Grow?

Parts of the Block

Sections are 2" wide pieces cut from panels and sewn to opposite sides of the center squares.

Center Squares are cut the width of the panels.

Panels are planted in rows of six 1½" wide strips and sewn together.

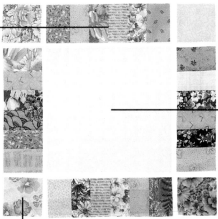

Cornerstones are 2" squares sewn to sections and then added to the sides of the center square, completing the block.

Parts of the Quilt

Edge Blocks are blocks cut in half to form triangles for the four sides of the quilt.

Corner Blocks come from one block cut in quarters.

Rainbow Borders are sections sewn together into long strips the width and length of the quilt top. Background strips are then added to both sides of the long strips, and sewn to all sides of the quilt.

Border Corner Squares are added to the Rainbow Borders.

Bed Quilt Borders are additional borders for larger quilts.

Yardage Charts

Patricia Knoechel

Wallhanging

Approximate Size 34" x 34"
Total blocks 8

	Yardage	Cut selvage to selvage from yardage or scraps
Different Prints for...		
8 Blocks & Rainbow Border	(9) ⅛ yd pieces	(2) 1½" wide strips from each
		(18) 1½" strips total
	or	**or**
	Assorted strips	(18) 1½" strips total
Planned Cornerstones		
1st Fabric	⅛ yd	(1) 2" wide strip
		(16) 2" squares
2nd Fabric	⅛ yd	(1) 2" wide strip
		(16) 2" squares
	or	
Or Scrappy Cornerstones	Assorted 2" wide strips	(32) 2" squares
Background	1⅛ yds	
Block Centers		Cut later
1st & 3rd Borders		(8) 2" wide strips
Border Corner Squares		Cut 4 squares later
Backing	1¼ yds	Or one piece 39" square
		(1) 6" strip for casing
Batting	40" x 40" piece	
	or packaged crib size	
Binding	½ yd	(4) 3" wide strips

"Mackie"

Baby Quilt

Approximate Size 47" x 47"
Total blocks 18

	Yardage	Cut selvage to selvage from yardage or scraps
Different Prints for…		
18 Blocks & Rainbow Border	(15) ⅛ yd pieces	(2) 1½" wide strips from each (30) 1½" strips total
	or	**or**
	Assorted strips	(30) 1½" strips total
Planned Cornerstones		
1st Fabric	⅛ yd	(2) 2" wide strips (36) 2" squares
2nd Fabric	⅛ yd	(2) 2" wide strips (36) 2" squares
	or	
Or Scrappy Cornerstones	Assorted 2" wide strips	(72) 2" squares
Background	1½ yds	
Block Centers		Cut later
1st & 3rd Borders		(8) 2" wide strips
Border Corner Squares		Cut 4 squares later
Backing	3 yds or one piece 52" x 52"	
Batting	52" x 52" piece or packaged twin size	
Binding	½ yd	(5) 3" wide strips

"Mackie"

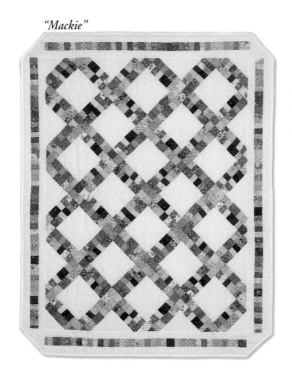

Lap Robe

Approximate Size 47" x 60"
Total blocks 24

	Yardage	Cut selvage to selvage from yardage or scraps
Different Prints for… 24 Blocks & Rainbow Border	(21) ⅛ yd pieces	(2) 1½" wide strips from each (42) 1½" strips total
	or	**or**
	Assorted strips	(42) 1½" strips total
Planned Cornerstones 1st Fabric	¼ yd	(3) 2" wide strips (48) 2" squares
2nd Fabric	¼ yd	(3) 2" wide strips (48) 2" squares
	or	
Or Scrappy Cornerstones	Assorted 2" wide strips	(96) 2" squares
Background Block Centers 1st & 3rd Borders Border Corner Squares	1⅔ yds	Cut later (10) 2" wide strips Cut 4 squares later
Backing	3 yds or one piece 52" x 65"	
Batting	52" x 65" piece or packaged twin size	
Binding	⅔ yd	(6) 3" wide strips

Sharon Woo

Twin Quilt

Approximate Size 61" x 99"
Fits 39" x 75" mattress
Total blocks 36

	Yardage	Cut selvage to selvage from yardage or scraps
Different Prints for…		
36 Blocks & Rainbow Border	(30) ⅛ yd pieces	(2) 1½" wide strips from each
		(60) 1½" strips total
	or	or
	Assorted strips	(60) 1½" strips total
Planned Cornerstones		
1st Fabric	¼ yd	(4) 2" wide strips
		(72) 2" squares
2nd Fabric	¼ yd	(4) 2" wide strips
		(72) 2" squares
	or	
Or Scrappy Cornerstones	Assorted 2" wide strips	(144) 2" squares
Background	2¼ yds	
Block Centers		Cut later
1st & 3rd Borders		(12) 2" wide strips
Border Corner Squares		Cut 4 squares later
Other Borders		
4th Border	⅞ yd	(7) 3½" wide strips
5th Border	1¼ yds	(8) 4½" wide strips
Backing	6 yds	
	or one piece 65" x 104"	
Batting	65" x 104" piece	
	or packaged queen size	
Binding	⅞ yd	(9) 3" wide strips

"Mackie"

Double Quilt

Approximate Size 82" x 107"
Fits 54" x 75" mattress
Total blocks 48

	Yardage	Cut selvage to selvage from yardage or scraps
Different Prints for…		
48 Blocks & Rainbow Border	(36) ⅛ yd pieces	(2) 1½" wide strips from each
		(72) 1½" strips total
	or	**or**
	Assorted strips	(72) 1½" strips total
Planned Cornerstones		
1st Fabric	⅜ yd	(5) 2" wide strips
		(96) 2" squares
2nd Fabric	⅜ yd	(5) 2" wide strips
		(96) 2" squares
	or	
Or Scrappy Cornerstones	Assorted 2" wide strips	(192) 2" squares
Background	2⅔ yds	
Block Centers		Cut later
1st & 3rd Borders		(14) 2" wide strips
Border Corner Squares		Cut 4 squares later
Other Borders		
4th Border	1½ yds	(8) 5½" wide strips
5th Border	2 yds	(9) 6½" wide strips
Backing	7½ yds	
	or one piece 90" x 115"	
Batting	90" x 112" piece	
	or packaged king size	
Binding	1 yd	(10) 3" wide strips

Loretta Smith

Queen Quilt

Approximate Size 87" x 112"
Fits 60" x 80" mattress
Total blocks 70

	Yardage	Cut selvage to selvage from yardage or scraps
Different Prints for…		
70 Blocks & Rainbow Border	(51) ⅛ yd pieces	(2) 1½" wide strips from each
		(102) 1½" strips total
	or	or
	Assorted strips	(102) 1½" strips total
Planned Cornerstones		
1st Fabric	½ yd	(7) 2" wide strips
		(140) 2" squares
2nd Fabric	½ yd	(7) 2" wide strips
		(140) 2" squares
	or	
Or Scrappy Cornerstones	Assorted 2" wide strips	(280) 2" squares
Background	3½ yds	
Block Centers		Cut later
1st & 3rd Borders		(16) 2" wide strips
Border Corner Squares		Cut 4 squares later
Other Borders		
4th Border	1¼ yds	(9) 3½" wide strips
5th Border	1½ yds	(9) 4½" wide strips
Backing	8⅛ yds	
	or one piece 96" x 120"	
Batting	96" x 120" piece	
	or packaged king size	
Binding	1¼ yds	(11) 3" wide strips

Ruth Griffith

King Quilt

Approximate Size 103" x 116"
Fits 76" x 80" mattress
Total blocks 84

	Yardage	Cut selvage to selvage from yardage or scraps
Different Prints for...		
84 Blocks & Rainbow Border	(60) ⅛ yd pieces	(2) 1½" wide strips from each
		(120) 1½" strips total
	or	**or**
	Assorted strips	(120) 1½" strips total
Planned Cornerstones		
1st Fabric	⅝ yd	(9) 2" wide strips
		(168) 2" squares
2nd Fabric	⅝ yd	(9) 2" wide strips
		(168) 2" squares
	or	
Or Scrappy Cornerstones	Assorted 2" wide strips	(336) 2" squares
Background	4 yds	
Block Centers		Cut later
1st & 3rd Borders		(17) 2" wide strips
Border Corner Squares		Cut 4 squares later
Other Borders		
4th Border	1½ yds	(10) 4½" wide strips
5th Border	1¾ yds	(10) 5½" wide strips
Backing	9¼ yds	
	or one piece 108" x 120"	
Batting	108" x 120" piece	
	or packaged king size	
Binding	1¼ yds	(12) 3" wide strips

Personalizing Your Garden

This versatile quilt can have all kinds of different themes and possibilities! Here are some suggestions. See page 66 for instructions.

Photo Transfer

How about a photo in the background center square?
Using special photo transfer paper, you can iron an image
from a favorite photo onto your background fabric.

Hand Prints

You could present "Nana" with a garden of her grandchildren's hand prints in primary colors.

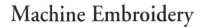

Machine Embroidery

Try this if you have a sewing machine that embroiders flowers, especially the large variety.

Friendship Quilt

Have family members sign their names to squares, or use those "memorial" T-shirts for the background squares. You could have your children draw something for that "special someone."

In one class, a quilter brought strips cut from her children's clothes which she had saved over the years. Of course, the strips were of various lengths, making panel sewing a challenge. What fun you will have poring over those scraps and what memories they will bring back!

17

Supplies

Fiskars Ruler/Cutter

6" x 24" ruler

6" x 6" ruler

Cutting Mat

Yarn

Floss

Neutral Thread

Invisible Thread

Scissors

Rotary Cutter

Walking Foot

Quilt Sew Easy™

Cellophane Tape

6" x 12" ruler

Square-Up

Stencil

Jaws™

Kwik Klip™

Clamps

Safety Pins

Binding Clips

Stiletto

Sew-Perfect™ or Magnetic Seam Guide

Quilter's Straight Pins

Disappearing Ink Pen

Quilter's Pencil

Pigma Pen

White Marking Pencil

Sewing Machine Needle

Embroidery Needle

Hand Sewing Needle

Techniques

Cutting Strips

Use a 6" x 24" plexiglass ruler, a large size rotary cutter with a sharp blade, and a gridded cutting mat. Use the mat's grid lines and the ruler's lines to ensure straight cuts. Cut strips from selvage to selvage. Yardage requirements are based on fabric at least 42" wide.

1. Check purchased fabric to see if it was torn from the bolt and is on the straight of the grain. Your first cut should straighten the edge and get rid of the "fuzzies."

   If it was cut rather than torn from the bolt, it may not be on the straight of the grain. However, when working with ⅛ or ¼ yard pieces, there is very little extra to waste in making a correcting tear. Open the fabric and see if the edge is straight. Your first cut should straighten the edge.

2. Place the folded fabric on the gridded cutting mat with the fabric to your right if you are right handed; reverse, if left handed.

3. Place the folded edge along a horizontal line, and match the raw or fuzzy edges along a vertical line.

4. If your ruler has a ¼" line, place it on the raw edge of the fabric, or use the grid lines of the mat.

5. Hold the cutter in one hand, and place the other hand on the ruler. Spreading your fingers, keep four on the ruler. Press your little finger firmly against the ruler's edge to keep it from slipping.

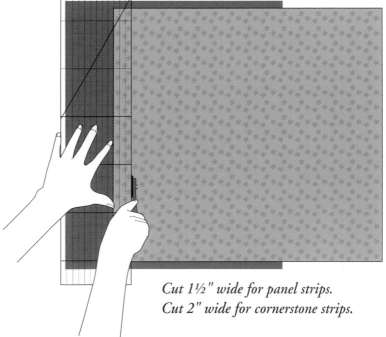

Cut 1½" wide for panel strips.
Cut 2" wide for cornerstone strips.

6. Expose the blade of the cutter and place it below the fabric next to the edge of the ruler. Begin cutting away from you while applying pressure to the cutter and to the ruler.

7. Midway along the ruler, stop cutting but do not lift the blade. Gently "walk" your ruler hand up the ruler, reapply pressure, and continue cutting until you reach other side of the fabric.

8. Lift the cutter and close immediately. Lay the cutter above the fabric so there will be no danger of cutting yourself or dragging the blade across the fabric.

9. Check the first strip for a bend at the fold. You may need to refold the fabric (not the strip) and make a trimming cut.

10. Cut the strips at the designated widths by placing the line of the ruler against the edge of the fabric and cutting.

11. If you cut strips from your "stash" of leftover strips of different widths, place the wider ones on the bottom. Stack as many as you can comfortably cut, being careful to have the grain of the fabrics parallel with the grid lines.

Do not use a crooked strip because it affects the panel of full strips and borders.

Cutting Cornerstones

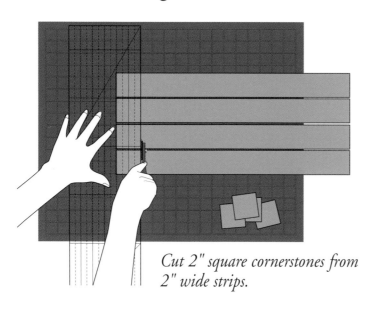

Cut 2" square cornerstones from 2" wide strips.

1. When cutting many squares, leave the strips in place in order to make multiple cuts.

2. Trim the selvage edge straight with the grid.

3. Move the ruler 2" and cut.

Cutting Cornerstones from Scraps

Stack and press several scraps consistent with fabric grain in order to avoid bias edges. Stack with the largest scrap on the bottom, graduating to smallest on top. Use the 6" x 6" ruler to cut 2" squares from stack of scraps.

Stitches per Inch

Use 15 stitches per inch, or 2 on machines with stitch selections from 1 to 4.

Seam Allowance

Sew an accurate and consistent ¼" seam allowance. Experiment to find a method that works for you. Items available include an exact ¼" foot made for your machine, a magnetic seam guide, masking tape, adhesive pad strip, and Sew Perfect™ Companion Guide which matches your needle position with a guiding strip fixed to the machine. It is important to feed the fabric into the machine so that the needle hits the fabric exactly and consistently ¼" from the raw edge.

Assembly-line Sewing

Save time and thread when sewing several paired pieces by butting one after another without cutting the thread or removing from the machine. Use the stiletto to help push patches under the presser foot and hold your seams flat as you sew over them.

Pressing

Using steam is a personal preference for advanced quiltmakers. Use a dry iron when indicated. If you choose to use steam, press carefully because steam can distort fabrics.

Use a gridded pressing mat.

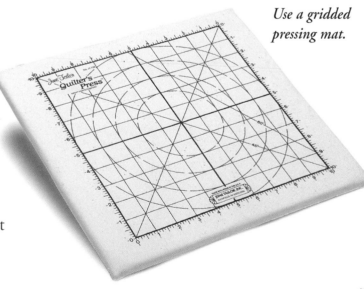

Setting the Seam

When "setting the seam," lay the sewn piece unopened on the ironing board or pressing mat. Lift and move the iron. Bring the dry iron straight down on the sewn seam. Do not aggressively push the iron along the stitching.

Directing the Seam Allowance

Based on the best construction plan, seams are pressed behind a specific fabric. When "setting the seam," lay the sewn piece on the ironing board or pressing mat with the specified fabric on top, and the seam away from you. "Set the seam," lift the top fabric, and press toward the seam. This pushes the seam allowance toward the upper fabric. Make sure there are no folds at the seam line.

Making the Blocks

Making the Panels

A panel is made of six 1½" wide strips. Use strips from yardage at least 42" wide. For more variety in the panels, particularly in the smaller quilts, cut 42" strips in half and mix up in two half panels. Half strips are also easier to press. If using scraps, combine strips of similar length.

Sewing Pairs Together

1. Divide the 1½" wide strips into two equal stacks. Place this many in each stack:

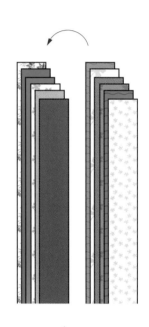

	Full Strips		Half Strips
Wallhanging			18
Baby			30
Lap Robe	21	or	42
Twin	30	or	60
Double	36	or	72
Queen	51	or	102
King	60	or	120

2. Place the stacks to the left of your sewing machine. Pair fabrics that look attractive together. Vary the colors, values, and textures, avoiding similar fabrics next to each other.

3. Flip the strip on the right to the strip on the left, right sides together.

4. Sew 15 stitches per inch using an accurate ¼" seam allowance. Match the top edges. The bottom edges may vary.

5. Do not remove strips from the machine or clip the threads.

6. Flip the next pair of strips right sides together.

7. Assembly-line sew all of the stacked strips into pairs.

8. Clip connecting threads.

Keep top edges even. ¼" seam allowance. 15 stitches per inch.

Bottom edges may vary.

Pressing Pairs Open

1. Place one pair on the pressing mat, with the top edge to the left. **Line up the strip with the grid on the mat.**

2. "Set the seam" by gently placing the iron on the stitching.

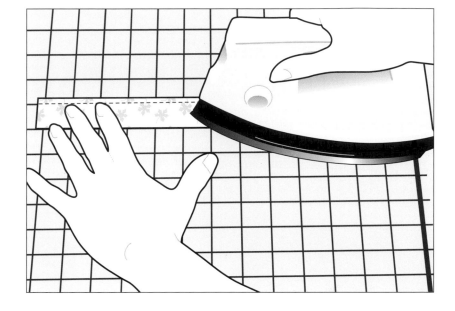

3. Lift open, and gently press against the fold.

4. Press open and stack all pairs.

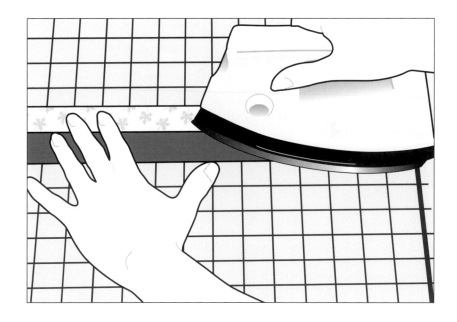

Sewing the Panels

1. To the left of your sewing machine, lay out three pairs of strips. Vary the colors and values.

2. Label them A/B, C/D, and E/F.

3. Stack a second set of three pairs, leaving an inch of the first pairs visible. Rearrange the second pairs when similar colors or values are next to, directly above or below each other.

4. Stack a third layer of pairs.

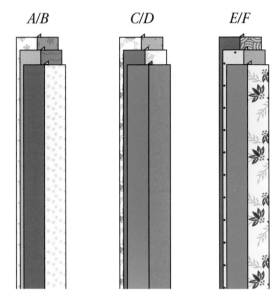

The pairs are ready to sew into panels.

Sewing Panels to Prevent Warping

To prevent warping, sew pairs together in the opposite direction.

1. Work with the top layer of pairs. Flip the C/D pair onto the A/B pair right sides together. Keep the top edges even.

2. Turn the pairs around in order to sew with the B strip on top. The ends of the A/B and C/D pairs may be uneven.

3. Sew the B and C strips together.

4. Do not remove pairs from the machine or clip the threads.

5. Assembly-line sew the remaining C/D and A/B pairs, with B on top.

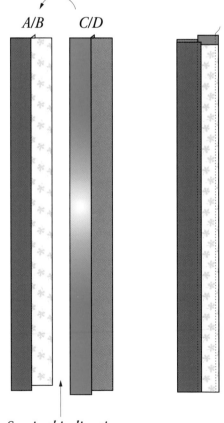

Sew in this direction.

6. Flip the E/F pair onto the A/B /C/D set, keeping the top edges even.

7. Turn the strips around in order to sew with the D strip on top. The edges may be uneven.

8. Sew the D and E strips together.

9. Repeat with all three pairs. Three panels are completed.

10. Continue stacking and sewing, three at a time, the number of panels for your size quilt.

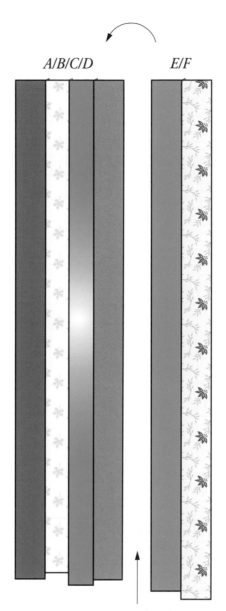

A/B/C/D   E/F

Sew in this direction.

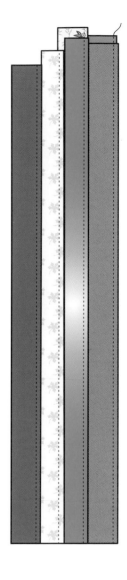

	Full Panels		Half Panels
Wallhanging			6
Baby			10
Lap Robe	7	or	14
Twin	10	or	20
Double	12	or	24
Queen	17	or	34
King	20	or	40

Pressing the Panels

1. "Set the seams" on the two unpressed seams. Keep the strips lined up with the grid as you press.

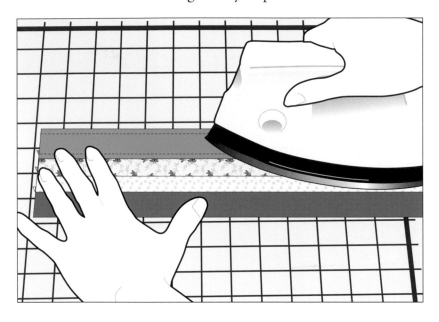

Place panel right side up on pressing mat with F across the top. Flip the two top strips to the wrong side and press the seam between D and E. Pull strips toward you and press seam between B and C. Do not pull or stretch the panel.

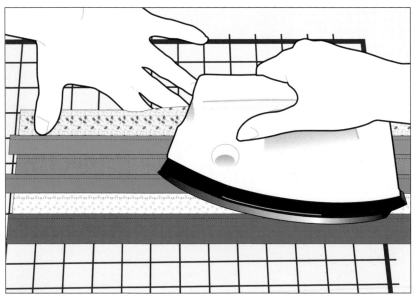

2. Turn the panel to the wrong side, with seams going away from you. From the wrong side, place the iron on the bottom strip. Lift the top of the panel with your free hand and push the iron away from you, pressing the seams in one direction.

3. Turn the panel over and check that there are no folds at the seams.

4. Press remaining panels.

Measuring the Panels

Place a 6" x 12" ruler on a panel to measure in several places – near each end and in the middle. Measure several panels.

The ideal measurement is 6½". Take an average and record here _____. Use this measurement later for the size of the block center.

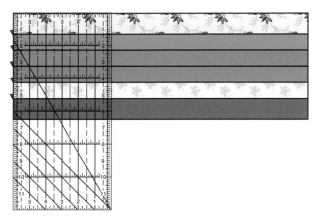

Cutting the Panels

1. Lay a panel on the cutting mat right side up, with the underneath seams going away from you. Place straight on the grid with the left edge beyond a vertical grid line.

2. Lay the ruler on the grid line. Rotary cut to trim and square the left edge.

3. Lift the ruler and measure over 2". Place a horizontal line of the ruler on a seam. Cut.

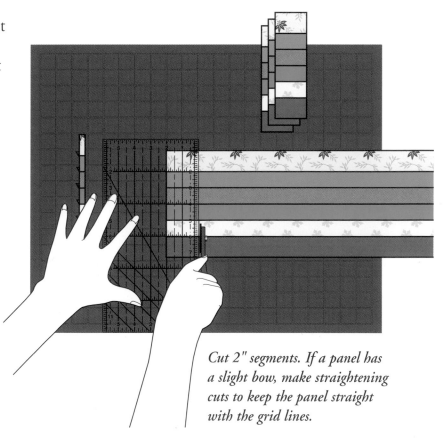

Cut 2" segments. If a panel has a slight bow, make straightening cuts to keep the panel straight with the grid lines.

4. Repeat, stacking sections in the same direction. Make straightening cuts when necessary. You should get 20 sections from each 42" panel, and 10 sections from each half panel. If necessary, make additional panels to get the required number of sections.

You need this many sections for your size quilt:

Wallhanging	52
Baby	100
Lap Robe	129
Twin	185
Double	237
Queen	334
King	394

5. Select a variety of sections and set aside for Rainbow Border. Set aside this many sections for the Rainbow Border:

Wallhanging	20
Baby	28
Lap Robe	33
Twin	41
Double	45
Queen	54
King	58

Did you get enough sections? Or do you need to make more?

Cutting Background into Center Squares

1. Place the folded background fabric on the cutting mat.

2. Trim the ragged edge straight.

3. Transfer the measurement of your panel width recorded on page 27: _____".

4. Cut the background fabric strips at that width, approximately 6½".

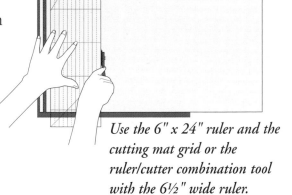

Use the 6" x 24" ruler and the cutting mat grid or the ruler/cutter combination tool with the 6½" wide ruler.

5. Leave several strips undisturbed on the mat. Turn the mat. Use the 6" x 24" ruler to trim the selvage edges and cut strips into squares.

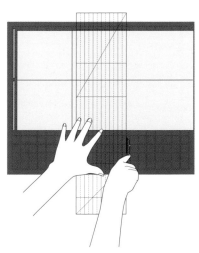

Or: Stack several layers of strips. Use the 12½" Square Up ruler to cut the strips into squares.

Cut according to your size quilt:

	Strips	Squares
Wallhanging	2	8
Baby	3	18
Lap Robe	4	24
Twin	6	36
Double	8	48
Queen	12	70
King	14	84

Adding Two Side Sections

*See page 66 if you want to decorate the center squares **before** adding the strip sections.*

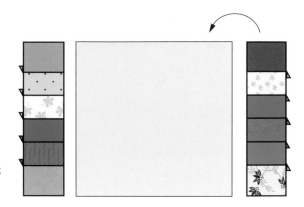

1. Lay out an equal number of sections on the left and right sides of the background squares.

2. Turn the sections in opposite directions so that the seam allowances on the right are going down, and the seam allowances on the left are going up. This will lock the seam allowances when blocks are sewn together.

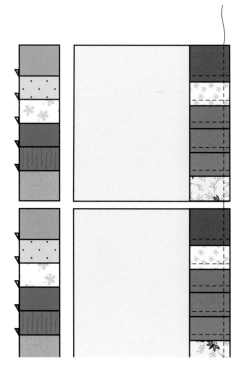

3. Flip the right section onto the background square right sides together and sew. Do not remove from machine or clip threads.

4. Assembly-line sew stacks.

5. Clip threads and restack.

6. Turn the sewn stack of blocks, and place next to the remaining sections.

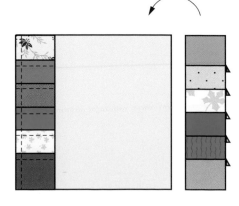

7. Repeat assembly-line sewing. Be sure the seam allowances are still pointed down.

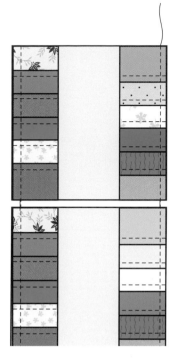

8. Press to set the seams.

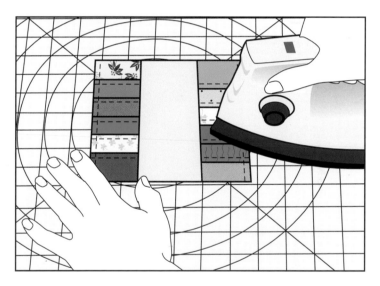

9. Open and press seam allowances away from the center square.

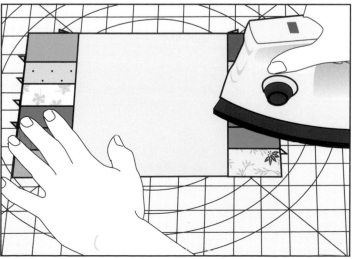

Adding the Cornerstones

1. Lay out a stack of 2" squares at each end of the remaining sections. Make sure the seams of the sections are all going the same direction.

You need this many in each stack:

	2 stacks of...
Wallhanging	16
Baby	36
Lap Robe	48
Twin	72
Double	96
Queen	140
King	168

Eleanor Burns

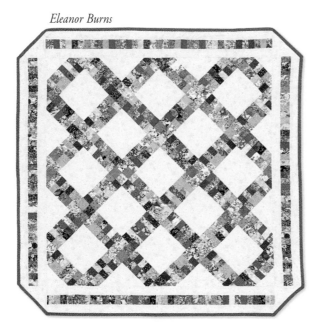

Scrappy Cornerstones: *Mix up your 2" squares so that different squares are sewn to the ends of identical sections.*

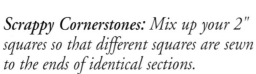

Eileen Murphy

Planned Cornerstones: *Place a stack of the first fabric at one end, and a stack of the second fabric at the opposite end.*

2. Flip the right cornerstone onto the end of the section and sew. Do not lift the presser foot nor clip threads.

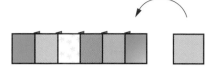

3. Assembly-line sew cornerstones onto all sections.

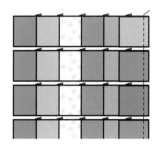

4. Clip apart. Restack.

5. Turn sections around.

6. Assembly-line sew remaining stack of cornerstones to sections.

7. Set the seams.

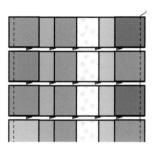

8. Fingerpress the cornerstone seams toward the section. Press with the iron.

9. Clip the connecting threads.

Adding the Remaining Sections

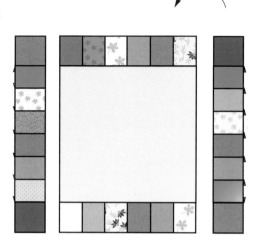

1. Lay out the stack of center squares with equal stacks of sections sewn with cornerstones. Place so that the seam allowances point down on the right, and up on the left.

   Planned Cornerstones: Be sure the same fabric is in opposite diagonal corners.

2. Flip the right section onto the center square and assembly-line sew.

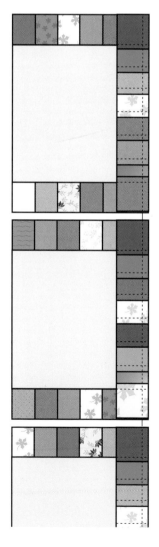

Friends are the cornerstones of life.

3. Clip connecting threads and restack in original order.

4. Turn the remaining stack so that the seam allowances point down. Flip and sew the remaining sections to the blocks.

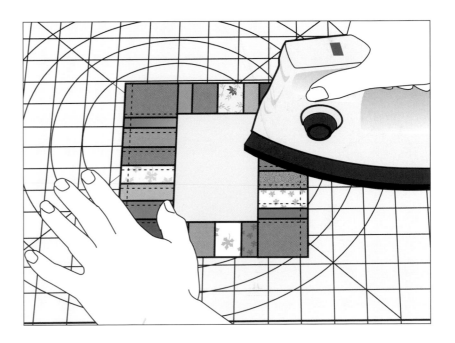

5. Set the seams with the sections on top.

6. Open and press seam allowances away from center square.

7. The seams are generally going the same direction around the block. This helps lock the seams when sewn to adjacent blocks.

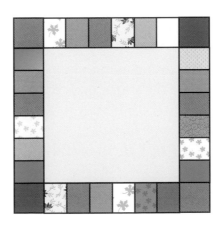

Optional Center Square Embellishment

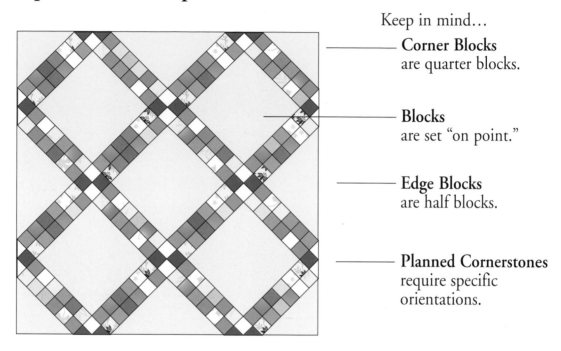

Keep in mind…

Corner Blocks are quarter blocks.

Blocks are set "on point."

Edge Blocks are half blocks.

Planned Cornerstones require specific orientations.

	Whole Blocks	Edge Blocks	Corner Block
Wallhanging	5	2	1
Baby	13	4	1
Lap Robe	18	5	1
Twin	28	7	1
Double	39	8	1
Queen	59	10	1
King	72	11	1

Stencil Marking

If you plan to "free form machine quilt" a non-directional design on the center square, trace the stencil onto the blocks now. If it is a directional design, mark the square after the quilt top is sewn together. See page 58.

Autographs/Pictures/Machine Embroidery

If you plan to personalize the quilt with writing, transferred photos, or other decoration, see page 66. You may wish to embellish only whole blocks.

Sewing the Blocks Together

Arranging the Blocks

1. Count out the blocks for your size quilt. There will be extra blocks which will later be cut and used along the edge and on the corners. Use the number of blocks and extras indicated for your size quilt.

	Blocks	Extras
Wallhanging	5	3
Baby	13	5
Lap Robe	18	6
Twin	28	8
Double	48	9
Queen	59	11
King	72	12

2. Lay out the blocks in the arrangement for your quilt. See following pages for block layouts.

Cornerstone Four-Patches

1. If you are using Scrappy Cornerstones, the blocks may be turned any direction. You aren't trying to make a pattern with the cornerstones.

2. If you are using Planned Cornerstones, turn the blocks so that the cornerstones form a four-patch where four blocks meet.

3. Rearrange blocks and substitute with the extras where the same fabric meets or until you are satisfied. **Do not sew the blocks together.**

4. Leave the layout in place while preparing the edge blocks.

Block Layouts

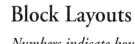

Numbers indicate how many blocks are in each row.

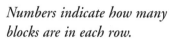

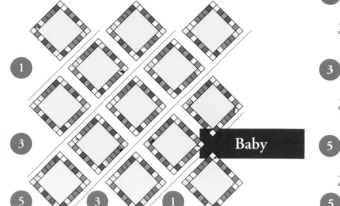

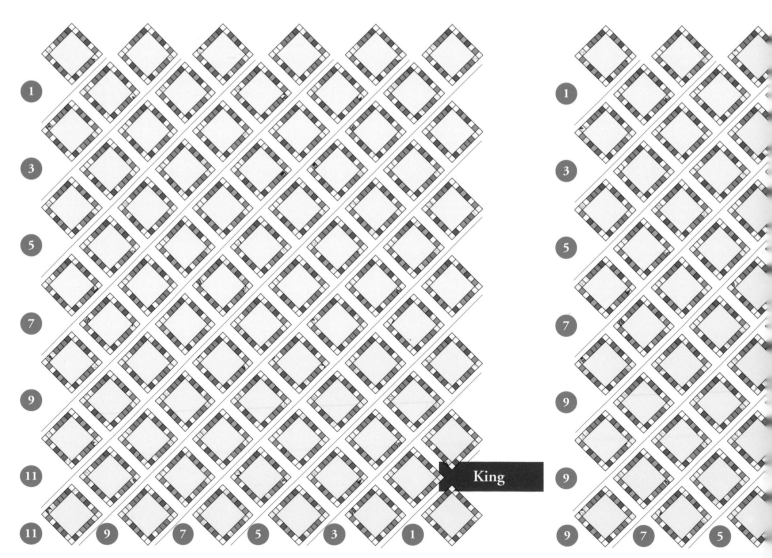

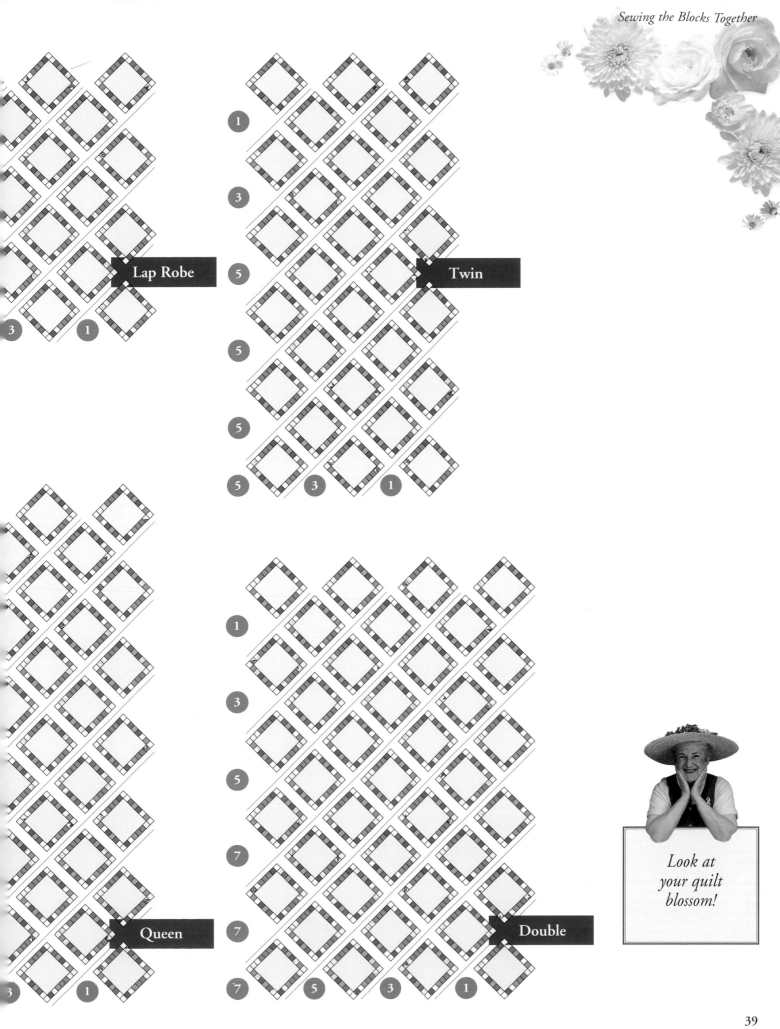

Lap Robe

Twin

Queen

Double

Look at your quilt blossom!

Making the Edge Triangles

Use the remaining blocks for your size quilt:

	Edge Blocks	Corner Block
Wallhanging	2	1
Baby	4	1
Lap Robe	5	1
Twin	7	1
Double	8	1
Queen	10	1
King	11	1

1. **Set aside the one block for the corner triangles. Do not cut yet!**

2. Lay the remaining blocks in place along the left edge and top edge of the layout.

   The orientation of Planned Cornerstones is important to form the four-patches.

   The half triangle from a block will be on opposite side of the quilt if your cornerstones are planned.

3. Lift out the top edge squares and fingerpress fold them in half as they will appear.

Fold in half—

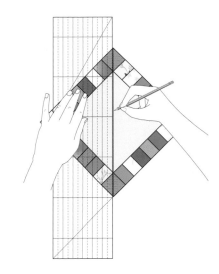

4. On the right side of the fabric, draw a diagonal line down the center from opposite corners. **Do not cut yet.**

5. Lift out the left edge squares and fingerpress fold them in half as they will appear.

6. On the right side of the fabric, draw a diagonal line down the center from opposite corners. **Do not cut yet.**

7. Assembly-line sew ⅛" on each side of line to help prevent bias edge from stretching. Press to set the stitching lines.

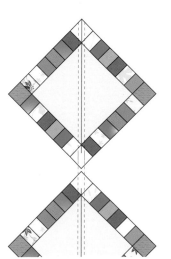

8. Cut the edge blocks on the diagonal line for the edge triangles.

9. Place the edge triangles back in the layout. If you are using Planned Cornerstones, check to see that the edge triangles complete the cornerstone four-patches.

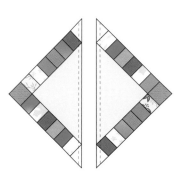

Making the Corner Triangles

1. Draw a diagonal line on the block reserved for the corners.

2. Draw a second diagonal line.

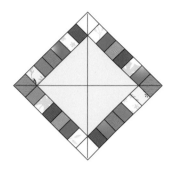

3. Sew ⅛" from both sides of both lines.

4. Press to set the seam.

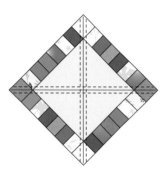

5. Cut on the diagonal lines. These four triangles are for the corners.

6. Place the corner triangles in the layout. If you are using Planned Cornerstones, check to see that the triangles complete the cornerstone four-patches.

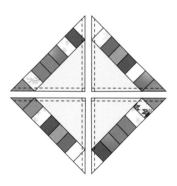

In quilting, "rose" is spelled r-o-w-s, but they don't smell as sweet!

Sewing the Rows Together

1. Working with one diagonal row at a time, pin and sew the pieces together, matching the seams.

2. After completing a row, replace it in the layout. Do not press these row seams.

3. Sew the rows together. Push the row seams in one direction, and push the row seams of the adjacent row in the other direction in order to lock the seams.

4. Add the corner triangles.

All pieces are now in place. Example: Lap Robe

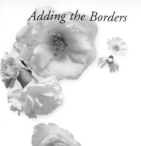

Adding the Borders

Trimming the Edges

1. Lay an edge of the quilt top on the cutting mat.

2. Use a ruler and rotary cutter to trim the edges straight. There is not a ¼" seam allowance beyond the point of the cornerstone.

Width

Length

Making the Rainbow/Background Border

1. **Measure across the cornerstones.** Do not measure at the edge because the edge blocks are cut on the bias and may have stretched even though they were stay stitched.

Record the length 82'14 "
and the width 58'½ "
of your quilt top.

2. Use the sections set aside from page 28. Make two stacks of sections with seams in the same direction.

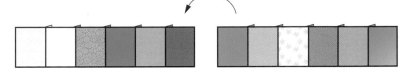

3. Flip and sew pairs and pairs of pairs until you have:

> two strips longer than your quilt length…

> …and two strips longer than your quilt width.

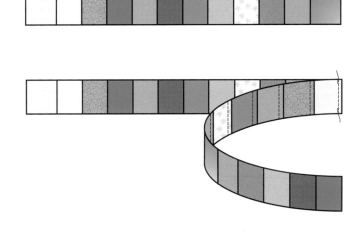

4. Press all the seams of each rainbow strip in one direction.

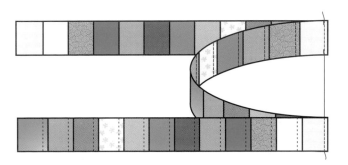

Example: Lap Robe

5. Lay each of the four rainbow strips on the quilt to confirm that they are slightly longer than the width or length of the quilt.

6. Use the cut 2" wide background strips for the first and third borders. Sew background strips together to the length of each of the four rainbow strips. Make two background strips for each of the four rainbow strips. *The Wallhanging and Baby sizes fit without piecing background strips.*

7. To avoid seams meeting at the same distance, shorten one strip by cutting off a portion.

No thorns in this garden, but watch the pins.

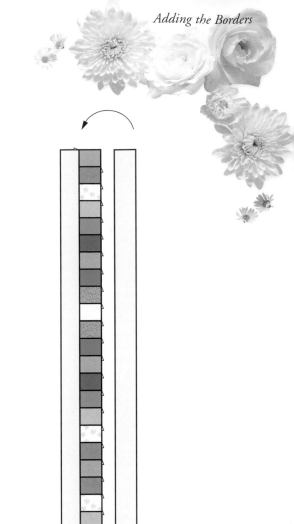

8. Working with one side of the quilt at a time, flip and sew the rainbow strip to a background border strip. The rainbow seams should be pointed down. Sew with the background strip underneath. Hold the strips together while sewing to keep them feeding at the same rate.

9. Press to set the seam with the background on top. Lift and press the seam to the background strip.

10. Flip and sew the remaining background strip to the rainbow strip. Sew with the rainbow strip underneath. Hold the strips together while sewing to keep them feeding at the same rate.

11. Press to set the seam with the background on top. Lift and press the seam to the background strip.

12. Trim each sewn border to the width or length of your quilt.

$\dfrac{59}{83}$

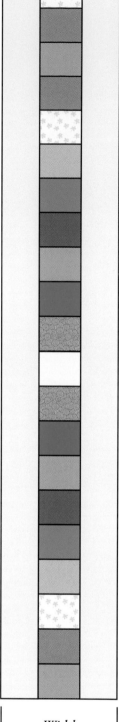

Rainbow Border Background Corner Squares

1. Measure and record the width of your border's three sewn strips _____" approximately 5".

2. Cut four background fabric squares the measurement of your border width.

Width

*Measure twice,
cut once.*

Sewing the Rainbow Border to the Quilt

1. Mark the middle of the borders and the middle of the quilt sides.

2. Match the middle of the sewn border to the middle of the side of the quilt. Right sides together, pin at the middle and at each end. Pin intermittently.

3. Sew the left and right side borders to the quilt.

4. Press the seam to the border.

Match ⟶

5. Sew a background square to each end of the top and bottom borders.

6. Match, pin and sew top and bottom borders to quilt.

7. The bed size quilts are now ready for additional borders.

Match

Eleanor Burns

Wallhanging, Baby Quilt and Lap Robe
Small quilts are now ready for the batting and backing. Turn to page 54.

Wallhanging, Baby Quilt, and Lap Robe with Angled Corners

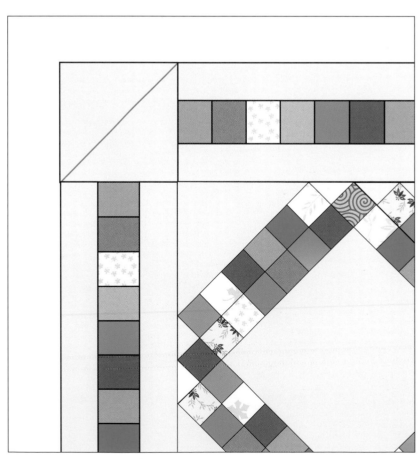

Because these small quilts do not have additional borders, the corners may be angled. If you want angled corners, draw a diagonal line on the right side of each border corner square.

Bed Quilt Borders
Adding the Fourth Border

1. Following the Yardage and Cutting Chart for your size quilt, cut the suggested number of strips.

2. Use a rotary cutter and ruler to trim away the selvages at a right angle.

3. Measure the length of the quilt down the center and left and right sides. If the measurements differ, take an average measurement.

4. Sew strips together end to end to make two sets of strips.

5. Sew this many strips together.

6. Cut the sets of strips to the average measurement.

Length		
	Strips	**2 sets**
Twin	4	2
Double	4	2
Queen	5	2½
King	5	2½

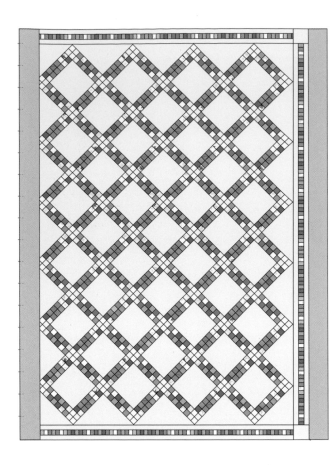

7. Place pins at the midpoints of the strips and pins at the midpoint of the quilt's left and right sides.

8. Place the border strips on the quilt, right sides together. Match pins at middle and both ends. Pin strips in place approximately every 3".

9. Sew with a ¼" seam allowance. Stretch or ease as necessary.

10. Set seams and press toward the fourth border.

11. Measure the width of the quilt, including the borders, across the top, center and bottom. If the measurements differ, take an average.

12. Sew this many strips together end to end to make two sets of strips.

Width		
	Strips	2 sets
Twin	3	1½
Double	4	2
Queen	4	2
King	5	2½

13. Cut the sets of strips to the average measurement.

14. Place pins at the midpoints and pin border strips on the quilt, right sides together. Sew with a ¼" seam allowance.

15. Set seams and press toward the fourth border.

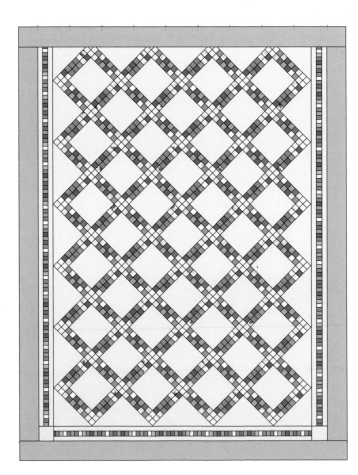

*Your top is done!
You got it made
in the shade.*

Adding the Fifth Border

Add fifth border in the same manner.

1. Sew strips together end to end to make two sets of strips.

2. Pin and sew side borders to quilt.

Length		
	Strips	**2 sets**
Twin	5	2½
Double	5	2½
Queen	5	2½
King	5	2½

3. Sew strips together end to end to make two sets of strips.

4. Pin and sew top and bottom borders to quilt.

Width		
	Strips	**2 sets**
Twin	3	1½
Double	4	2
Queen	4	2
King	5	2½

Finishing the Quilt

Preparing the Backing

Follow the yardage chart for your size quilt.

1. Measure and record the length of your quilt top._____"

2. Using that number, measure down the length of the backing yardage and add 4". Put a pin to mark the spot.

Length of Quilt Top + 4"

3. From the pin, measure down the rest of the fabric to make sure you have enough to make two or three pieces that same length, depending on your size quilt.

4. Cut a nick close to the pin and tear across the grain.

5. Selvages do not give and will pucker if you do not remove them. Cut a nick at the selvage on both sides and tear along the length of the fabric to remove.

6. Place the pieces right sides together. Pin.

7. Sew a ½" seam down the length of the fabric.

8. Press the seam allowance to one side.

If you have less backing yardage than listed on your chart, use the width of the quilt as the beginning measurement. Then your seams will be horizontal across the back.

Machine Quilting

If you plan to Free Motion machine quilt a directional design on the center square, trace the stencil onto the quilt top before layering. See page 58.

Layering

1. Place the backing with the wrong side up on a large surface. Smooth out the wrinkles. Clamp or tape.

2. Lay the batting on top and smooth any creases. Reclamp or tape to stabilize.

3. Place the quilt top with right side up on the batting, centering it so that the backing and batt are showing on all sides.

4. Straighten the borders in all directions.

Squaring the Corners and Pinning

The following steps help to make the quilt look straight on the bed or wall. This method controls the borders, and lets you adjust any excess fabric you may have within the quilt.

1. Place a 12½" Square Up ruler in one corner of the quilt. Adjust the quilt so that the seams touch the ruler's edge on two sides.

2. On the opposite two sides of the ruler, place long straight pins.

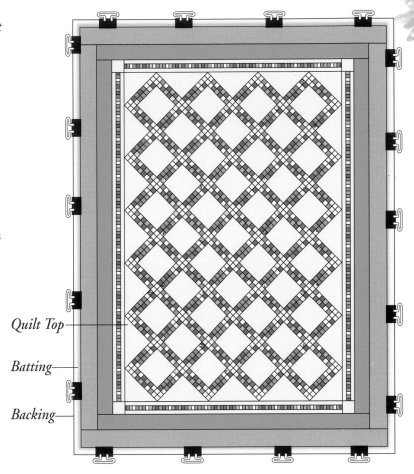

Quilt Top

Batting

Backing

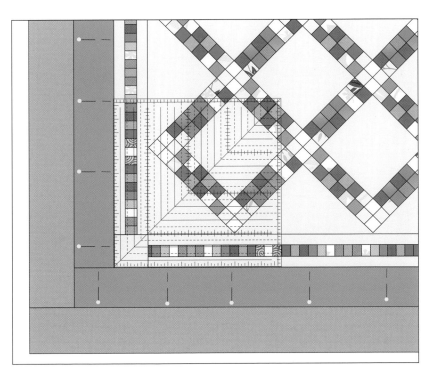

Pinning Technique

The fast and easy way to close and open safety pins is using a Kwik Klip pinning tool. Insert the point of the pin through all layers of the quilt, and take a ½" "bite."

Bring the point of the pin up through the quilt onto the Kwik Klip between the notches. Use the index finger to push the head of the pin down over the point to close it.

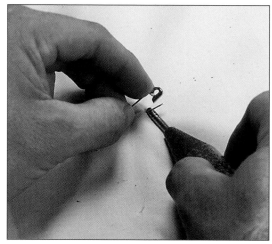

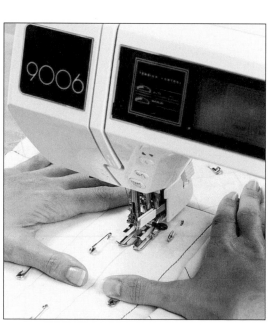

3. Safety pin through all layers in the border.

4. Move the ruler to the next border, adjust seams and safety pin through all layers of the border. It is not necessary to straight pin on opposite sides on this corner.

5. Repeat for all borders on all corners.

6. Safety pin the remaining sections of the borders.

7. Place safety pins in the sections along the sides of the background squares.

8. Remove the straight pins, clamps or tape. Trim backing and batting, leaving two inches on all sides.

Testing Your Stitch

1. Put on or engage your walking foot. Set the stitch length to 3 to 4 mm or 8 to 10 stitches per inch.

2. Make a "sandwich" of batting between layers of fabric.

3. Thread the machine with regular or invisible thread and test the stitching. You may have to reduce the top tension, particularly with invisible thread, or change the stitch length.

Stitch in the Ditch

1. Beginning at one corner, roll the quilt diagonally to the middle row of sections. Secure the roll with quilt clips or Jaws. Roll the opposite corner toward the center leaving a 6" space.

2. Slide the rolled quilt under the presser foot. Insert the needle in the beginning of the seam line, and lock the stitch. Sew to the end of the seam, lock the stitch, and clip threads.

3. Move the quilt to the next "ditch." Lock the stitches, and sew to the end of the seam.

4. Continue "stitching in the ditch," unrolling that portion of the quilt as needed, and rerolling the other portion until all the seams have been sewn diagonally on that portion.

5. Reroll that section and unroll the other to the next seam to be quilted. Turn the roll around so that the sewn portion is on the left. Continue stitching, unrolling and rolling until all seams are quilted on the diagonals.

6. "Stitch in the ditch" around the borders.

7. Place the quilt on a flat surface, and hand baste through all layers close to the raw edges of the quilt.

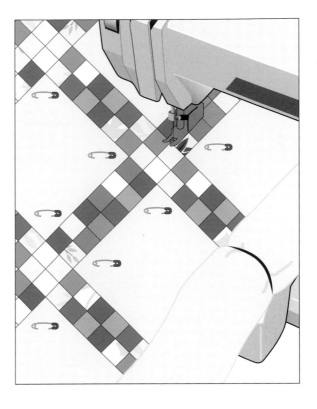

Continue stitching until all seams are quilted.

Free Motion Quilting

After stitching in the ditch, you may "free motion quilt" a design in the background square.

1. Choose a stencil that can be sewn in a continuous line and is 5" x 5" so that it will fit within the background square.

   ❖ If the design is non-directional, it can be marked on the background square before or after the print sections are added.

   ❖ If the design is directional, trace it on the background squares after the blocks are sewn together, but before layering with backing and batting.

2. Trace the stencil with a fine line pencil or special pen that washes out. Do not use a pen that disappears unless you want to mark and quilt one square at a time.

3. Thread the machine and bobbin with regular thread that matches the background square.

4. Trace the stencil on a scrap piece of background fabric. Make a test "sandwich" to become comfortable with the pattern before starting on the quilt.

5. Drop the feed dogs or cover the feed dogs with a protective plate. Place a darning or embroidery foot, spring needle, or darning spring on your sewing machine.

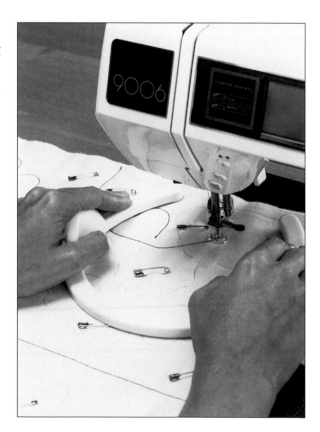

6. Slide the quilt under the darning foot at one of the marked squares. Insert the needle at the starting point, and lower the presser foot.

7. Bring up the bobbin thread. Lock the stitch. With the needle down, place your hands flat around the pattern forming a triangle. Use the "Quilt Sew Easy™" designed to help hold the layers taut. With both hands, move the quilt under the needle following the pattern.

8. Upon reaching the starting point, lock the stitches, pull up the bobbin thread and clip.

Stippling

Stippling is random stitching on background areas to add dimension to the quilt. Use the same machine set-up.

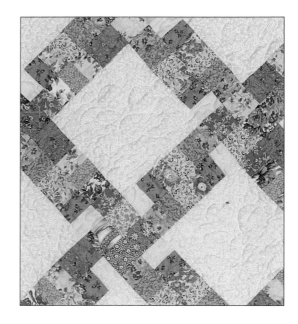

1. Insert the needle at the edge of the background square.

2. Raise the needle, and bring the bobbin thread to the surface. Pull up the slack in the thread. Lock the stitches.

3. Sew a few stitches in one direction, then curve around and back toward the beginning making a loop. Remove safety pins as you sew.

4. Before you reach the point where you began, curve back toward where you started without crossing previously sewn stippling.

5. Continue making loops until you fill the area. Move toward the edge and lock the stitches. Clip loose threads.

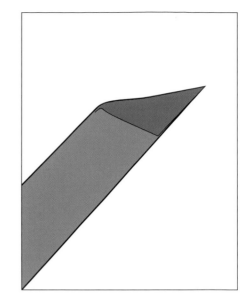

Sewing the Binding

Follow the Yardage and Cutting chart for the number of 3" wide strips for your quilt. Cut off the selvages at a right angle.

1. Sew the binding strips right sides together end to end. Press the seams open.

2. Fold one end diagonally wrong sides together. Press.

3. Fold strips in half lengthwise wrong sides together. Press. At the folded end leave about 6" open. Machine baste together less than a ¼" along the raw edges to prevent the binding from warping.

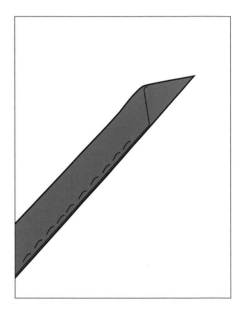

4. Lay the quilt on a flat surface. Pin the unbasted end of the binding midway on the right side of the quilt. Match the raw edges. Lay the binding around the edge of the quilt. If a seam in the binding comes to within 2" of any corner, remove the pin and shift the binding.

5. Pin the diagonally folded end to the quilt top. Roll or fold the binding so as not to wrinkle or tangle it.

6. Use a walking foot and regular thread that matches the binding. a ¼" seam, and 10 stitches per inch.

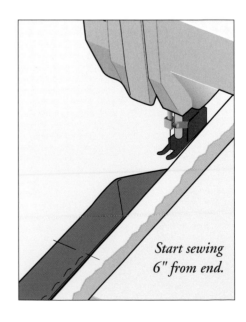

Start sewing 6" from end.

7. Begin stitching approximately 6" from the diagonal fold. Match the raw edges of the binding to the raw edges of the quilt top.

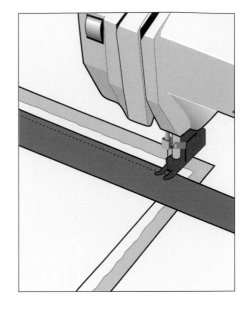

Mitering a Square Corner

1. Stop stitching ¼" from the corner. Sink the needle into the fabric and lift the presser foot.

2. Pivot the quilt at a right angle. Put the presser foot down. Reverse the stitching past the raw edges of the quilt top. Lift the presser foot.

3. Pull the quilt toward you. Pull the binding straight up. Fingerpress a diagonal fold at the corner.

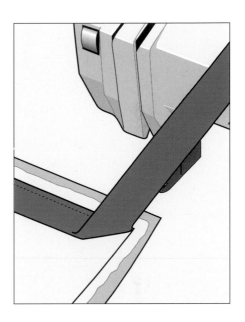

4. Fold the binding over the miter. Match the raw edges of the binding to the quilt top. Lower the presser foot and sew forward onto the binding.

5. Continue to each corner and repeat the miter. Sew to where it is pinned, within 6" of the starting point.

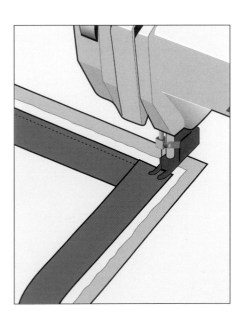

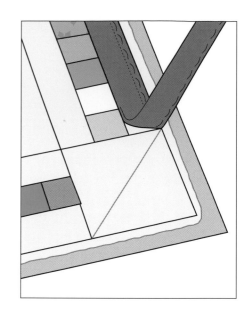

Mitering an Angled Corner

1. Stop stitching ¼" from the penciled angle. Sink the needle into the fabric and lift the presser foot.

2. Pivot the quilt at a 45 degree angle. Put the presser foot down. Reverse the stitching past the raw edges of the quilt top. Lift the presser foot. Pull the quilt toward you.

3. Pull the binding straight up. Finger press a diagonal fold at the corner.

4. Fold the binding over the miter. Match the raw edges of the binding to the drawn line. Lower the presser foot and sew forward onto the binding.

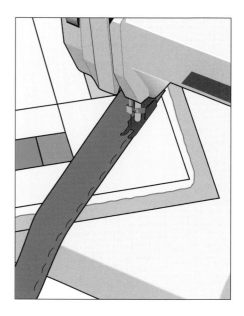

5. Continue to each corner and repeat the miter. Sew to where it is pinned, within 6" of the starting point.

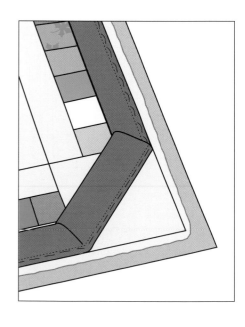

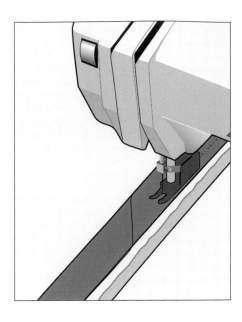

Joining Ends with an Upholstery Tuck

1. Trim the excess binding on the diagonal, leaving approximately 3" to tuck in.

2. Insert into the diagonal fold.

3. Pin and continue sewing to the starting point. Backstitch and clip threads.

4. With an old blade in your rotary cutter trim backing and batting to within ¼" of the quilt top edge to help fill the binding.

   If you intend to put a hanging sleeve on the back, see page 64.

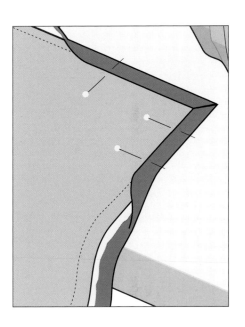

5. Fold the binding to the back of the quilt just past the stitching. Tuck the miters in place at the corners. Pin the binding in place.

6. You can now "stitch in the ditch" from the right side by machine.

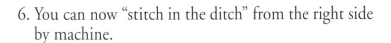

To stitch by hand, use little hair clips called "Goodies" to hold the binding in place. Hand slip stitch the binding to the back.

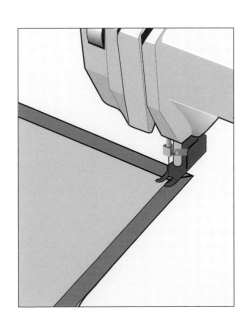

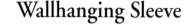

Wallhanging Sleeve

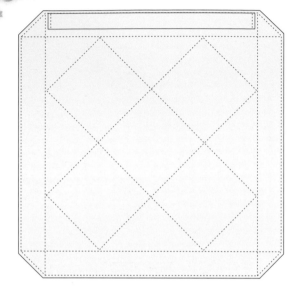

There are many ways to hang a quilt on the wall, such as cute little wooden clamps, quilt presses, and push pins. But the sleeve or casing is the most universal.

1. Measure and record the width of the quilt. _____"

2. Cut a strip to match the backing at that measurement and 6" wide.

3. Approximately 1" from one end fold the raw edge wrong sides together toward the middle to form a hem. Finger press and fold again. Sew the hem. Repeat at the other end.

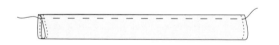

4. Fold in half lengthwise and press, wrong sides together.

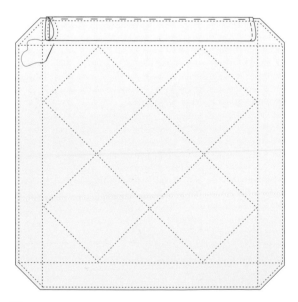

5. Machine baste the raw edges together less a ¼" from the edge.

6. After the binding is sewn on, and the backing/batting have been trimmed, pin the sleeve at the top of the quilt on the back. Re-sew, following the binding seam.

7. Hand sew the folded edge of the sleeve to the back of the quilt.

The Label

The label identifies the pattern, maker, date, and the state in which it was made. Some are quite elaborate, while others are plain and simple. It can be written on a fabric label, using a permanent marker, or embroidered with floss and a needle directly onto the fabric. Hand stamps are available with embossed titles which can be filled in with a permanent marker.

Other pertinent information may be added, if the quilt was made for a specific person, for a special occasion, or made with clothing worn by someone. For instance, the legend might tell that a quilt was made by grandma using her old aprons, or dresses, or someone's baby clothes. The purpose of the legend is to preserve the unique history of your quilt.

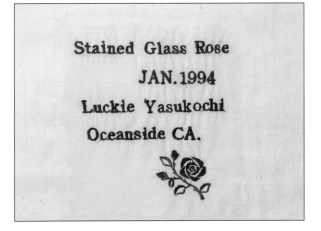

"The Legend"

A quilt ain't a quilt 'til the legend's on the back,

'til the "PPPD's" in place.

That's pattern, person, place and date:

put it on, don't hesitate,

with something no one can erase.

You can write it,

you can type it,

you can embroidery,

bead or stamp.

You can even French Knot it 'til your hands get a cramp.

Just remember what Mackie said:

"Don't you put it on your bed

'til that Legend's on the back."

Decorating your Garden

Mackie

Photo Transfer

The light colored fabric for the background of this block lends itself perfectly to this method of decorating with a theme. Photo quilts make perfect anniversary, family reunion, birth or wedding gifts.

1. Use tightly woven, 100% smooth cotton. Do not pre-wash. Cut the background square as described on page 29.

2. Select your favorite photos. Arrange as many pictures as possible on a plain piece of 8½" by 11" paper.

3. Purchase photo transfer paper available in quilt shops. Instructions may vary. Follow the directions for your particular brand.

4. Have a mirror image color copy made of the photographs on the coated side of the transfer paper. Cut the images apart.

5. Place the square on the pressing mat or electronic press. Press to remove wrinkles, creases, lumps or bumps.

6. Center the transfer on top of the square, image side down, and press on a cotton setting for 15 seconds while applying heavy pressure. Do not use steam.

7. While paper is still hot, lift one corner to check if transfer has occurred. If so, quickly peel off paper. If not, continue to press for another 10 seconds, and then remove paper, starting at the corner.

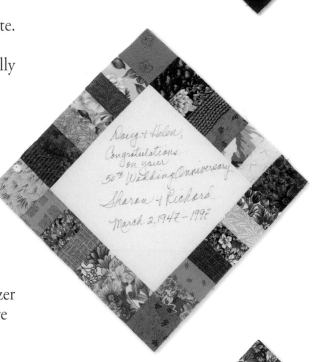

Children's Hand Prints

1. Use a permanent, machine washable fabric paint. (Children should be supervised by an adult.)

2. Cut the background square to size. Pre-wash fabric and lay on shirt board, cardboard, or other disposable work surface.

3. Shake well, and squeeze paint on paper plate.

4. Place child's hand in paint and then carefully make print on fabric.

5. Dry flat for twenty-four hours.

6. Fabric may be washed after seventy-two hours in cool water and air dried.

Written Messages

1. Cut the background to size.

2. Stabilize by "fusing" the waxed side of freezer paper to the wrong side of the center square fabric, or place on a piece of sandpaper.

3. Write the message with a fine point, permanent marking pen. Make certain that the writing is at least 1" from the edge to allow for seam allowance and margins.

Machine Embroidery

1. Cut background oversized to fit into embroidery hoop.

2. Place a piece of stabilizer under the piece of fabric.

3. Center the design on point. Stitch.

4. Pull off the stabilizer, and press.

5. Cut background square to size.

Applique

Any applique pattern can be used. These patterns are included for your use.

1. Sew the blocks together. Add a framing border.

2. Cut background fabric to your desired border width in place of the Rainbow Border. Complete as much applique as you can before adding borders to top.

Sewing the Flowers

1. Place non-woven fusible interfacing on pattern, smooth side up. Trace flowers with a fine, permanent pen.

2. Place interfacing with traced patterns on the fabric with "dotted" fusible side against right side of fabric. The smooth side of the interfacing is on top. **Do not press.** Pin.

3. Sew **on the lines** with a small stitch, or 20 stitches per inch.

4. Trim each piece ⅛" away from the lines.

5. Cut a small slit in the interfacing.

6. Gently turn right side out through the cuts.

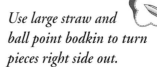

7. Pull out corners with stiletto.

Use large straw and ball point bodkin to turn pieces right side out.

Making the Vines

1. Cut 1½" wide bias strips to the desired length. Press in half right sides out.

2. Pencil in placement lines for the vines.

3. Stitch the bias strip in place ¼" from the raw edge.

4. Flip the folded edge over the stitches, concealing the seam. Pin in place. Blindstitch in place with invisible thread, or matching thread and twin needle.

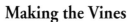

Applique Patterns

Finishing

1. Position the flowers on the background borders at the ends of the vines. Firmly press flowers in place.

2. Stitch around the outside edge with invisible thread and a blind hem stitch, or contrasting thread and a blanket stitch.

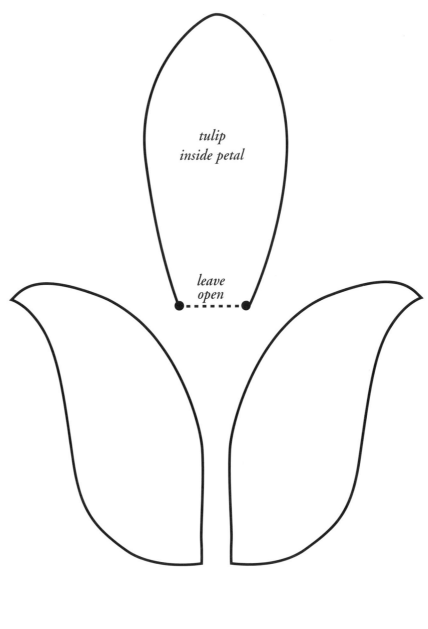

tulip inside petal

leave open

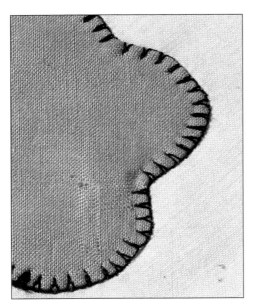

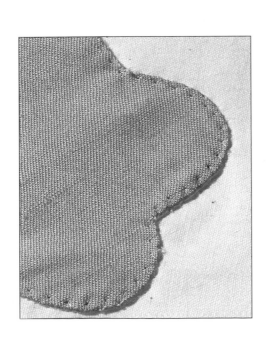

flowers

Acknowledgements

I would like to acknowledge the following…

Elsa Arrigo Erickson, a childhood friend, who died of breast cancer in 1995, and to Claudell Leverich, a beautiful rose in His garden, who dropped her petals in 1997.

Also Margie Hansen and Ruth Hakala who are survivors.

But most of all I would like to acknowledge

Eleanor Burns for being a "Fairy Goldmother" and granting all my wishes.

Loretta Smith for her genius in transcribing my words into meaning.

Ruth Griffith for the use of her computer, culinary skills, and millinery expertise!

Sharon Woo for bringing Nana's Garden to my attention.

To all my quilting friends/students for their enthusiasm and support.

*Sharon Woo
Designer of the
Nana's Garden Pattern*

I met Sharon seven years ago in a quilting class when we both lived in Garden Grove, CA. We've been best buds ever since. It was when she moved to San Jose, CA with her husband, Richard, and had a lot of time on her hands that she developed Nana's Garden. She is an avid quilter and teaches Quilt in a Day's methods in the bay area.

Index

Photo transfer paper is available in quilt shops,
or may be ordered directly from:
Quiltmakers
9658 Plano Rd
Dallas, TX 75238

Order Information

Quilt in a Day books offer a wide range of techniques and are directed toward a variety of skill levels. If you do not have a quilt shop in your area, you may write or call for a complete catalog and current price list of all books and patterns published by Quilt in a Day®, Inc.

Easy

Quilt in a Day Log Cabin
Irish Chain in a Day
Bits & Pieces Quilt
Trip Around the World Quilt
Heart's Delight Wallhanging
Scrap Quilt, Strips and Spider Webs
Rail Fence Quilt
Flying Geese Quilt
Star for all Seasons Placemats
Winning Hand Quilt
Courthouse Steps Quilt
From Blocks to Quilt
Nana's Garden Quilt

Applique

Applique in a Day
Dresden Plate Quilt
Sunbonnet Sue Visits Quilt in a Day
Recycled Treasures
Country Cottages and More
Creating with Color
Spools & Tools Wallhanging
Dutch Windmills Quilt

Intermediate to Advanced

Trio of Treasured Quilts
Lover's Knot Quilt
Amish Quilt
May Basket Quilt
Morning Star Quilt
Friendship Quilt
Kaleidoscope Quilt
Machine Quilting Primer
Tulip Quilt
Star Log Cabin Quilt
Burgoyne Surrounded Quilt

Snowball Quilt
Tulip Table Runner
Triple Irish Chain Quilts
Bears in the Woods
Jewel Box Quilt

Holiday

Country Christmas
Bunnies & Blossoms
Patchwork Santa
Last Minute Gifts
Angel of Antiquity
Log Cabin Wreath Wallhanging
Log Cabin Christmas Tree Wallhanging
Country Flag
Lover's Knot Placemats
Stockings & Small Quilts

Sampler

The Sampler
Block Party Series 1, Quilter's Year
Block Party Series 2, Baskets & Flowers
Block Party Series 3, Quilters Almanac
Block Party Series 4, Christmas Traditions
Block Party Series 5, Pioneer Sampler

Angle Piecing

Diamond Log Cabin Tablecloth or Treeskirt
Pineapple Quilt
Blazing Star Tablecloth
Schoolhouse Quilt
Radiant Star Quilt

Quilt in a Day®, Inc. • 1955 Diamond Street, • San Marcos, CA 92069
Toll Free: 1 800 777-4852 • Fax: (760) 591-4424
Internet: www.quilt-in-a-day.com • 8 am to 5 pm Pacific Time